Young Artists of the World™
Nepal

Chandra Bahadur Ale's Painting:"Simple Living"

Jacquiline Touba, Ph.D. and Barbara Glasser

in collaboration with the IACA World Awareness Children's Museum

The Rosen Publishing Group's

PowerKids Press™
New York

The young artist's drawing was submitted to the International Youth Art Exchange program of the IACA World Awareness Children's Museum. You are invited to contribute your artwork to the museum.
For more details, write to the IACA World Awareness Children's Museum, 227 Glen Street, Glens Falls, NY 12801
Acknowledgments: M. Sitaula, Sishir Shrestha.

Published in 1997 by The Rosen Publishing Group, Inc.
29 East 21st Street, New York, NY 10010

First Edition

Book Design: Erin McKenna

Photo Credits: p.4 © AP/Wide World Photos; pp. 7, 8,15,16, 20 © V. Clevenger/H. Armstrong Roberts, Inc.; p.11 © Buddy Mays/International Stock Photography; p.19 © George Hunter/H. Armstrong Roberts, Inc..

Touba, Jacquiline.
    Nepal: Chandra Bahadur Ale's painting "Simple Living" / by Jacquiline Touba and Barbara Glasser
        p.   cm. — (Young artists of the world)
    Summary: Using a painting by a Nepalese boy as illustration, discusses what life is like in the country of Nepal.
    ISBN 0-8239-5103-0
    1. Nepal—Social life and customs—Juvenile literature. 2. Children's art—Nepal. 3. Child artists—Nepal. [1. Nepal—Social life and customs. 2. Children's art.] I. Glasser, Barbara. II. Ale, Chandra Bahadur, ill. III. Series.
    DS493.7.T68 1997
    954.96—dc21
                                                                  96–39804
                                                                     CIP
                                                                     AC

Manufactured in the United States of America

Contents

"*Namaste!*"

In Nepal we fold our hands in front of our faces and say "***namaste***" (nah-mah-STAY). This is how we say "hello" or "goodbye." We may say this to someone at any time of the day as a sign of **respect** (ree-SPEKT).

Namaste! My name is Chandra Bahadur Ale. I live in **Nepa**l (neh-PAHL), which is a country in Asia. I have two older brothers, two older sisters, and a younger sister. We enjoy spending time together. We also like to visit our **relatives** (REL-uh-tivz).

Chandra Bahadur Ale

◀ The people of Nepal greet each other with respect.

5

The People

The first people of Nepal came from India and Tibet. We speak **Nepali** (ne-pah-LEE). This is the official language of Nepal. But other languages are spoken as well.

In Nepal, there are two religions: Hinduism and Buddhism. They are an important part of everyday life in Nepal. People go with their families to both Hindu shrines and Buddhist temples for ceremonies and celebrations.

The people of Nepal are friendly and they respect each other. My country is known as the home of peace and wisdom.

The people of Nepal speak a language called Nepali. ▶

My Country

Nepal is in the middle of Asia. It is south of Tibet and surrounded on three sides by India. Nepal has almost every kind of landscape, from rain forests, to deserts, to icy mountains. The famous **Himalaya Mountains** (him-ah-LAY-ah MOWN-tinz) are in my country. They are often called the "Home of the Gods." People from all over the world come to my country to climb the Himalaya Mountains. People also come to see Mount Everest. It is the highest point in the Himalayas and in the world.

Kathmandu (KAT-man-DOO) is the capital of Nepal. I live near Kathmandu in a town called **Lalitpur** (LA-lit-POOR).

◀ Nepal is home to the Himalaya Mountains and Mount Everest.

Chandra's painting shows Nepal's Himalaya Mountains.

9

A Lucky Thing

When I was seven years old, a lucky thing happened to me. I had the chance to travel to the country of Hong Kong with one of my uncles. I went to school there for almost three years. I learned how to read, write, and draw at school in Hong Kong.

After my trip to Hong Kong, I returned to Nepal. There I went to a **boarding school** (BOR-ding SKOOL) in Lalitpur. I was also chosen to be a scout leader. I did a lot of drawing with my scout troop. One of my drawings won an award and it was sent to the 1988 Olympics in Seoul, Korea.

Chandra had the chance to study in Hong Kong. ▶

My Painting

Here is my painting of my aunt and uncle. They are weaving mats on their farm. Their farm is near Lalitpur, next to the mountains. My aunt and uncle grow crops such as corn, wheat, and rice on their farm. They also raise cows, buffaloes, and goats.

During the summer I visit my aunt, uncle, and cousins. I help them by taking care of the animals. I also plant and work on the crops. My cousins help too. My aunt and uncle weave mats and baskets after they finish their farm work.

Chandra's painting shows how his aunt weaves mats.

◀ I have painted my aunt and uncle weaving baskets in front of their house.

Mats

The mats and baskets that my aunt and uncle weave are made of bamboo. Bamboo is a strong grass that can grow up to ten or twelve feet tall. My uncle is using a *khurpa* (KER-pah) to cut the bamboo. My aunt will use the pieces of bamboo to weave a mat. Mats are used to make fences or sheds at my aunt and uncle's house. If there are any mats left afterwards, they are sold at the market.

Sometimes **traders** (TRAY-derz) stop at the farm. They want to know if there are any mats or baskets for sale. In the city, the mats are used by street **merchants** (MER-chentz). They sit on the mats and sell their goods.

Mats are made of bamboo, which is strong and thick. ▶

Baskets

The baskets that my aunt and uncle make can be used for many things. Farmers use them to carry water jugs. In some villages high in the mountains, people walk to a well to get their water. They carry the jug full of water in a basket back to their homes. These people carry the baskets on their backs. **Sherpas** (SHUR-pahz) are people who live in the Himalaya Mountains and use the baskets to carry food and other supplies for people who climb the mountains. In 1953, a Sherpa named Tenzing Norgay and another man named Sir Edmund Hillary were the first two people to reach the top of Mount Everest.

◀ These Sherpas are taking a break.

Chandra included a basket in his painting that is just like the sherpas' baskets.

17

Clothing

Chandra's uncle wears clothing much like the men in Katmandu.

My aunt and uncle are wearing the clothing of Nepalese farmers. They make all of their own clothes.

My aunt wears a shirt called a *cholo* (CHO-low) and a skirt called a *sari* (SAH-ree). My uncle's shirt is a *daura* (DAW-rah). He wears loose pants and a jacket with buttons on the side. My uncle's hat is called a **topi** (TOE-pee). The designs on the topi tell us that my uncle is a farmer from Lalitpur.

Men who visit Kathmandu from the farms wear their topis. This ▶ way other people know which towns they've come from.

The Farm

My aunt and uncle's home has a roof made of a hollow plant called cane. Cane grows in the Kathmandu valley. The rest of the house is made of concrete, wood, and stones. During the winter, it can get very cold in the mountains. The only form of heat in many houses is a small fire. This fire is used for cooking too. We also use heavy clothing and blankets to keep us warm.

The small building next to the house is where the corn and hay are kept. And the farm animals live in the small building in the back.

The buildings in Chandra's painting have cane roofs.

◀ Farm buildings can be made of strong cane, wood, or stone.

21

Education in Nepal

I go to a boarding school, so I live at my school. My classes are from ten in the morning to five in the evening, five days a week. My cousins go to school in the city. They have to walk to school every day from their farm. It is a very long walk.

In some villages in the mountains, there aren't any places for kids to go to school. Sometimes teachers hold classes under a tree or in a field.

Not long ago, some people thought that girls should not go to school. But my younger sister goes to school. Today, we know it's important for everyone to learn as much as we can about our country and the world.

Glossary

boarding school (BOR-ding SKOOL) A school where students live during the school year.

cholo (CHO-low) A woman's shirt.

daura (DAW-rah) A man's shirt.

Himalaya Mountains (him-ah-LAY-ah MOWN-tinz) A large chain of mountains that runs through Nepal.

Kathmandu (KAT-man-DOO) The capital city of Nepal.

khurpa (KER-pah) A cutting tool with a curved blade.

Lalitpur (LA-lit-POOR) A town near Kathmandu.

merchant (MER-chent) A person who buys and sells goods.

namaste (nah-mah-STAY) The word for hello and goodbye in Nepali.

Nepal (neh-PAHL) A country in central Asia.

Nepali (ne-pah-LEE) The language of Nepal.

relative (REL-uh-tiv) A person who belongs to your family, such as a cousin or an uncle.

respect (ree-SPEKT) To admire someone.

sari (SAH-ree) A woman's skirt.

Sherpa (SHUR-pah) A person who helps climbers in the Himalaya Mountains.

topi (TOE-pee) A man's cloth hat.

trader (TRAY-der) A person who buys and sells different goods.

Index